EXPLAIN

YOURSELF!

HOW TO DO EXPLAINER VIDEOS
THE RIGHT WAY

EXPLAIN
YOURSELF!

HOW TO DO EXPLAINER VIDEOS
THE RIGHT WAY

BEN MARVAZI

Explain Yourself!
How To Do Explainer Videos The Right Way

Front Cover Design by Promoshin.com
Book Pages & E-book Design: Velin@Perseus-Design.com

ISBN: 978-0-692-83688-0

TABLE OF CONTENTS

INTRODUCTION

D o you remember the first time you used the Internet? Driving back from Circuit City with your 30-pound Gateway in the trunk, past gas stations offering fuel for $1.08, unboxing the behemoth in the office your family would soon dub the "computer room," waiting four and a half minutes for it to boot up, tapping your foot impatiently while your eardrums endured *that sound...*

BEEP BOOP BUM BAP BIP BOP WAH WUHHHH, WAH WUHHH, SKREEEEEEEEEECH

Close your eyes and visualize that moment in your own life. Wait, actually, open your eyes. You're gonna need them to read this next section. (Isn't text so *inconvenient?*)

It was hard to imagine, back in the early days of the World Wide Web, that video would one day be the language of the Internet. Back when we watched Geocities websites load one pixel at a time, and the only visuals were obnoxious .gifs of dancing babies. Back then, businesses woke up to the notion that they would need a website to survive. Now, they're waking up to the idea that a text-based website that would have suited them just fine in 1998 won't cut it anymore.

Enter the age of the Explainer Video.

You've seen them around. Colorful visuals accompanied by a voiceover describing that new social media site, or that organic granola bar startup, or that genius Kickstarter invention. Over the past ten years or so, these videos have become ubiquitous to the point of necessity. You might be in the unfortunate position of looking around at your competitors and finding you're the only one on the block still trying to pitch your business in a paragraph.

If you're the kind of person who...

○ **Looks at your site analytics and wonders how to turn all those visitors into customers**

○ **Is launching a startup or a crowdfunding campaign to attract attention to your new idea**

○ **Is currently staring at your homepage wondering where you're gonna put your shiny new video**

This book is for you.

Where do these videos come from? Why do you need one? Who makes them? How much do they cost? What goes into producing them? Do they really help, or are they just another trend?

This book will answer all those questions and more. The information you'll find inside these pages is based on my experience running one of the highest-volume explainer video production companies, as well as verifiable research from around the web. I'll give you the skinny on web video marketing, as well as insider tips and tricks for navigating the thicket of video companies that have sprung up over the past few years.

So, let's start with the most important question...

CHAPTER ONE
WHY THE HECK DO I
NEED ONE OF THESE?

If an explainer company cold-calls you, you can bet that their sales pitch will include some variation on the idea that "nobody reads anymore." I'm guilty of whipping this line out myself from time to time. It invokes a bleak image of our 21st century world, a world of shrinking attention spans and a growing need for instant gratification.

The truth, as usual, is more complicated and less pessimistic. While it's probably true that the average person today is less inclined to read five paragraphs about your company than their pre-Internet ancestors, I don't think we can blame it on a decrease in intelligence. Instead, I think it's caused by an increase in the speed with which we access information.

Back when we paid ten cents for the newspaper, or had to wait five minutes to load a webpage, we had an investment in that content. It was worth our time to stay and read. Now, in a day and age when a click will take us on to something else in a microsecond, we don't have any skin in the game. In other words, your content used to earn attention by virtue of being difficult to get to. Now, you've got to earn attention in a better way.

Millions of businesses have discovered that video is that better way. Here are eight reasons why:

1. We learn better from video. When I was in grade school, my favorite days were always when the teacher decided to give up on lecturing, wheeled in one of those TV carts, threw on a Ken Burns documentary, and let the screen do the talking.

I'm not a neuroscientist, but I know there's a reason I forget my Euclidian Geometry but can remember every line from *Willy Wonka and the Chocolate Factory*. *Willy Wonka* was entertaining, and stimulated my visual and auditory senses all at once. Visuals and sounds stimulate interest, and interest stimulates learning and retention.

Let's put it this way: would your potential customers rather read the book or see the movie?

2. Video adds credibility. Just like shrinking attention spans, another 21st century malady that gets blamed on the Internet is loss of trust. This one might be a little more accurate. Years of spam, scams, adware, malware, hacks, hoaxes, worms, and viruses have made the web-using public increasingly wary of the unknown.

If the goal of your business is to get people to give you their contact info, sign up for a quote, buy a product, subscribe to a service, or donate money, then you're inevitably going to rub up against these trust issues.

> Having a video proves that you've invested time and money into your idea. It shows that you're serious.

Video is a great way to alleviate these fears. Anyone with a computer can create a website, throw up some descriptive text, and wait for foolish users to fall into their trap. Having a video proves that you've invested time and money into your idea. It shows that you're serious.

Does video, on its own, prove you're legit? Of course not, but it certainly helps.

3. Video lowers your opportunity costs. I had a client who was launching a small business and spent half an hour on the phone with every lead, pitching his idea and answering all their questions. His entire work day was spent on these calls. He didn't have time to do any of the other work required to get his business off the ground. On top of that, what was happening to all those leads that he didn't call?

Video was the perfect solution for this client. Instead of spending so much time on the phone, he could just point them to his homepage, where an explainer video gave them a succinct overview of his pitch. Interested clients could call for more information, and the ones who weren't interested moved on at no cost to him. He freed up time to focus on growing his business, and as it grew, he could expose his idea to more and more people without having to hire extra sales staff.

4. Video increases conversions. According to a 2014 research study by Aberdeen[1], websites that used video in their content marketing had conversion rates averaging 4.8%, while websites without video converted at only 2.9%. Anecdotal evidence from all over the web claims that sites like Dropbox increased conversions up to 20% after uploading their first explainer video. In fact, the Dropbox website was nothing but an explainer video and a sign-up box for several years.

> Websites that used video in their content marketing had conversion rates averaging 4.8%, while websites without video converted at only 2.9%.

Of course, these stats are going to vary on a case-by-case basis, and will depend on a number of factors, like the quality of your video, your sales strategy, etc. But if there was a possibility that you could increase your conversions up to 20% by making a relatively small investment, why wouldn't you?

---

[1] Analyzing the ROI of Video Marketing, Aberdeen Group, 2014

5. Everybody else is doing it. I know. This is exactly what my mother scolded me for saying when she found out I ditched school to go to the beach. "If all your friends jumped off a bridge, would you?" But hey, sometimes the movements of the crowd are worth following.

According to that 2014 Aberdeen study, video was the number one most used web marketing material of the businesses surveyed. 95% of top performing companies used video, compared to 66% using curated content like blog posts. Video also beat out white papers, web events, infographics, and (uh-oh) ebooks.

There's a reason explainer videos are more popular than ever. If they weren't working, they would have gone the way of the pop-up ad and the custom mouse cursor.

6. Video can be shared. One of the biggest advantages of video is that our current Internet infrastructure is built for sharing it. Every major social media site has a video sharing feature, and video discovery engines like YouTube are among the most visited sites in the world.

With a video representing your company, every one of your customers' social media profiles becomes a potential vehicle for advertising. And if you create a particularly humorous or engaging video, you give your company a shot at going VIRAL.

You probably won't, but the *possibility* is there. So why not buy the Powerball ticket?

7. Video improves SEO. The algorithms Google uses to determine your website's rank in their results can seem as mysterious as dark matter. They are so mysterious that digital marketing agencies will charge you thousands of dollars to figure out how to get your site to the front page. But this much is clear: having video on your site increases your PageRank, which in turn improves your ranking not only on Google, but on YouTube as well. And I don't need to tell you what a better Google or YouTube ranking can do for your business.

8. Video is Versatile. I'll go into more detail later in this book about all the different ways you can use video. But here's a preview, courtesy of explainer video aficionado Bill Shakespeare:

> Video. How can I use thee? Let me count the ways.
> I'll post you on Facebook, Twitter, and Instagram
> Send you in emails (pray they're not marked as spam)
> I'll use you as an aid in my business pitch
> And turn my newsletter more content-rich
> Make a landing page for you, to generate leads
> Replace my "about me," (which nobody reads)
> Gain attention for my Kickstarter campaign.
> (and when it gets funded, pop the champagne)
> Put you on the monitor at my trade show booth
> For you, Video, are so versatile, and that's the truth.

So, video seems like a worthwhile investment. But how much should you invest?

CHAPTER TWO
THE FELLOWSHIP OF CHA-CHING

For a first time buyer, figuring out the cost of an explainer video can feel like an expedition through uncharted wilderness. The current production market has prices ranging from $25 to $25,000 and up, and the reasons for this disparity are often totally opaque.

So allow me to guide you on a journey across the epic landscape of explainer video production. In the end, it will be up to you to find a price point that suits your business. But until then, pack your things, kiss your family goodbye, and set off with me on an adventure.

First stop...

The Slippery Swamp of Self-Production. The lowest cost option for creating a video is to do it yourself. However, a low sticker price doesn't account for all of the labor you'll need to put in. If you don't have the writing, illustrating, animating, or recording skills necessary for video creation, and you don't have hundreds of hours to devote to learning professional-level animation software, then your best bet will be to use a cloud-based DIY animation platform.

There are several companies that offer this service, and they usually charge a monthly fee for use, plus additional charges for exporting files and removing their company watermark. These fees will start somewhere around $20 a month. You'll have to learn their tools, use their pre-set characters and assets, dedicate time to the project, and the resulting video will probably be depressingly adequate. In addition, anyone familiar with the platforms will be able to recognize their trademarks in your video.

> **Best for:** Personal or internal-use videos, making videos just for fun, or if you need to create videos in such a high volume that you can't afford other options.

The Fearsome Forest of Freelancers. Freelancers are individuals who offer their services independent of larger production companies. They will post their abilities on various freelancer sites, and their prices will generally range from $100 to $1,500 (or more).

Somewhere out there is a freelancer who is dedicated to client satisfaction, answers every phone call, and produces remarkable, artistic animated videos. Finding that freelancer is as unlikely as finding an unsigned Picasso at an estate sale, but they're probably out there somewhere—maybe playing cards with Bigfoot and Elvis. That perfect freelancer would probably not be too happy about what I'm about to say.

Hiring a freelancer is a huge gamble. You don't have a way to verify the quality of the work you'll receive. They have a reputation for being unresponsive. There is no guarantee that they won't run off with your deposit. There is no one to complain to when things go sour. There is no accountability.

The other issue with freelancers comes by virtue of them being an individual. Whereas a full-service company has scriptwriters, creatives, designers, illustrators, animators, and project managers at your disposal, a freelancer can probably only take on a portion of these responsibilities.

Which, in some cases, will be just fine. In most cases, you'll need something more.

> **Best for:** If you can't afford a full-service production company, have a lot of your own creative ideas, don't care about timeframe, and have the time and patience to micro-manage a project.

The Green Pastures of Full-Service Production. Most production companies, including mine, fall into this category. Our services range in price, usually starting around $1,000. Personally, I like to keep my company's services affordable for all sizes of business, so our prices peak at around $2,500. Other companies offering similar services will charge up to $10,000.

These companies will offer everything you expect from a business-facing corporation: support, accountability, a team of animators providing relatively quick turnaround speeds, incentives, sales, and additional services.

The most important thing to do when researching a company of this size is to view their portfolio. You might expect that the quality of their output will directly correlate with the cost of the service, but this isn't always the case. Some of these companies will even be contracting out to freelancers, or using those DIY production platforms, under the guise of employing skilled labor. Often the only difference between a company charging $1,000 and a company charging $10,000 will be where their workforce is located.

Obviously, the quality of the services and products delivered by these companies will vary widely. Later in this book, I'll provide a list of questions to ask when you're doing your research, so hopefully you'll be able to judge for yourself before handing over your deposit.

> **Best for:** Most businesses, excluding Fortune 500 companies with unlimited marketing budgets.

The Elysian Fields of Elite Production. Alas, we reach the top of the heap. These are extremely low-volume, extremely high-cost companies. They only take on big-name, highly funded clients. Their costs can range from $10,000-$25,000 and up. They will most likely send a consultant to your office, take you out for a steak dinner, and charge it to their American Express platinum card.

Some of these companies produce videos with extraordinary artistic vision, Oscar-worthy animation, original scores, and sound design. If you're a Fortune 500 company looking to produce a national TV commercial, they might be your best bet. If you're anyone else, their services are probably overkill.

Some of these companies will charge the same price as those Oscar-worthy companies, but provide the same level of service as production houses charging less than half the cost. These companies set astronomical prices in the hopes of baiting big name clients, but their end-products are no better than average. Remember, just because you're paying more doesn't mean you're getting more.

Best for: Recent lottery winners, Rockefellers, and oil barons.

One last stop on our journey, weary traveler. We're going to pay a visit to the mythical animal that is live action production.

CHAPTER THREE
LIVE ACTION, A WHOLE DIFFERENT BEAST

The costs I've been quoting thus far have all referred to animated production. Some companies in every range will also provide live action explainer production, or even operate exclusively in that field.

Live action production is worlds apart from animated production. The difference in labor is immense, and this is reflected in the cost. Unless you want to take your iPhone camera around your office and do it yourself (which I don't recommend), a live action video will cost you at least $3,000 to $5,000, and there is no upper limit, with many companies charging $30,000 to $50,000 or more.

The costs are so much higher because live action production is significantly more complex than animated production. I'll illustrate this by walking you through a standard live action production process.

Pre-Production

Script. Just like in animation, a team of creatives and a professional writer will help you come up with the content of the video. Live action writing is significantly more challenging, however, as it requires dialogue, scene description, and camera direction. If you've ever seen a bad movie, you know that poor dialogue can absolutely ruin a film, and that good writing is hard to pull off—so you're going to want to make sure you hire an experienced screenwriter.

Storyboard. Again, like animation, the creative team will draw up a storyboard for the producers to refer to. The producer will use the storyboard to make a detailed plan to secure all of the locations, equipment, and props you require.

Locations and Materials. Each location will need to be rented in advance, at a cost, or you might need to hire a set builder to create a location for you. Most equipment, such as cameras, lighting, and microphones, will be rented as well if your production company doesn't have a stock of their own. Props will need to be bought, built, or rented. All rentals will require insurance.

Permits and Insurance. Permits are required for filming in every major city. In many places, acquiring these permits can be challenging and expensive. Special insurance is also required to protect your crew and actors in case of accidents.

Casting. Good actors don't come cheap, but they are a necessity. Because of the cost of talent, you might be tempted to act in the video yourself or call in a favor from your cousin who played Oliver Twist in the middle school play. But bad acting will devalue every other part of the production and make your business look bad. It is absolutely crucial to cast carefully.

Scheduling. The producer and their team will then schedule shooting days. They will take into consideration the availability of the cast and crew, as well as the locations. If you have outdoor locations, weather will also need to be considered.

Production

Food and Transportation. You're going to need a big crew for your shoot, and for each day of shooting, your production company will be responsible for providing transportation for your cast and crew, as well as food. Your video is going to take at least a day to shoot, and usually longer, depending on the number of locations, scenes, etc.

Rehearsal and Prep. If you've ever visited a set or helped a friend with their film school projects, then you know that preparing each shot, rehearsing with the actors, and shooting every angle of every scene takes exponentially longer than you actually see in the finished project. Hollywood feature films, for example, usually require at least three months to shoot.

Lighting and Cinematography. As the cast is rehearsing, a crew member known as a "gaffer" will set up lighting for each scene. Depending on the size of the production, a cinematographer might also be on set.

Shooting. Your director will call "action" and begin the arduous shooting process. A script supervisor will need to be present to call out continuity errors (clocks displaying the wrong time, props moving between scenes, etc.). Sound recordists will record the audio. During the shoot, all digital video and audio files must be stored and organized diligently to ensure an efficient editing process. At the end of the day, hopefully there will be enough material to send to the editor.

Post-Production

Editing. After production has wrapped, the real work begins. An editor will take the mountains of footage collected during the shoot and start splicing together scenes. One scene typically has three or four angles, so that means each scene will be compiled from at least three or four separate takes. The editor will sync the audio to these scenes using special software.

Sound design. After the edit has been approved, a sound designer will need to mix and master the existing audio and add in sound effects. In a proper live action production, every footstep, chair creak, and gust of wind will need to be put in during post-production. The sound designer will usually be culling these effects from premium sound effects libraries, but they may need to create some effects themselves, which is called "foley."

Color correction. After the sound, the video will need to be color-corrected. This requires using special software to make the colors in the video more realistic and aesthetically pleasing.

Visual Effects. This can be as minimal as adding your logo and phone number to the frame, or as extensive as doing actual CGI special effects, but it is always necessary.

Finally, the video is ready for you, the client, to review. Then there's always...

Reshoots. If you notice something that's not quite up to your liking, you'll need to go all the way back to production and repeat, praying that your actors haven't gotten a haircut or gained weight in the months since the initial shoot.

So with all of these skilled laborers and added costs, live action production of any respectable quality is usually reserved for higher budgets. But it definitely has value, and is something to keep in mind.

Alas, our journey across this great countryside has ended. It is now time for the greatest adventure of all to begin. You must look inward, examine your own priorities, and determine what the value of a video is for *you*.

CHAPTER FOUR
THE MAGIC
NUMBER

Buying an explainer video is a lot like buying a car. Except that you're not allowed to test drive it. And you're partially responsible for designing and building it. And you don't know how well it will perform.

Okay, buying an explainer video is nothing like buying a car. But somehow you still have to decide whether you need a Camry or a Corvette.

This is not a decision to be made impulsively. It's important to remember that a web video for your business should be seen as an investment. If you choose wisely, you'll see an increase in sales, conversions, or whatever metric you're using to measure your success. If you choose unwisely, you can waste time, waste money, and potentially even hurt your brand and reputation. Hurting your brand doesn't just mean less business now—it can mean decreased interest for years to come.

Video Is An Investment

Good Video	Bad Video
Increased Sales & Conversions	Wasted Time
Increased Credibility	Wasted Money
Increased Brand Awareness	Damaged Reputation

With that in mind, here are some questions you can ask yourself to determine what price point will suit your needs.

How much time can I invest? In general, the less you pay, the more involved you'll have to be in the video production process to ensure a good outcome. There are extremes on both ends. Self-production, of course, requires 100% involvement. The most expensive companies might cash your check and tell you to sit back, relax, and wait for your video to be delivered on a silver platter.

Every other service will fall somewhere in between. Working with a freelancer will probably require a large amount of creative input, follow up, and patience. Some full service production companies will only act to facilitate the production, with you in the director's chair, and you'll need to take the time to be very specific about every part of the video. Some companies will have a creative staff that can relieve some of this burden for you. More experienced companies will have more streamlined processes with fewer speed bumps. Less experienced companies might still be figuring things out.

So take a look at your calendar. If you only have free time for fifteen minutes every other Wednesday, you'll probably want to invest in a company that can shoulder more of the load. If you've got the time, and the vision, then save some cash and devote yourself to your video.

How much detail do I need? Sometimes the difference between small and big-budget production options will be the level of detail in the animation. How important is it that the characters mouths move along with the voiceover, or that each of their limbs are rigged and move constantly and separately, or that their walk cycles are realistic? How important are the added flourishes that make each frame more visually interesting?

In other words, if the script and message are exactly the same, how important is it that the animation is incredibly detailed? Some audiences won't know, or care about, the difference. Some will.

How important is customer service? Often, a huge factor in why one company costs more than another is how much customer support they offer. I don't need to tell you how frustrating poor customer service experiences can be. Remember, you're going to be stuck with these guys for at least a few weeks. In a creative and collaborative process like video creation, good customer service with reliable contacts and staff that are available to address your needs will often lead to a better product.

Would you prefer to pay a little more in order to have a support staff you can call for status updates, revisions, and payment questions, instead of working with an email-only operation? Would you prefer to work with a project manager or creative director whose sole responsibility is client satisfaction, or deal with animators directly? Try to minimize your frustration by choosing a company that will put your needs first.

How much liability am I willing to take on? Remember, you're going to be entrusting these companies with large sums of money. How important is it to you that this money is refundable?

Some production companies will offer a no-questions-asked, 100% money-back guarantee. Some will offer this only under certain conditions. Some will keep your down payment no matter what the circumstances. You'll need to decide upfront how much a plan B is worth to you.

How many people will see it? We'll get into detail about all the different uses for explainer videos later in the book, but you should be aware that some use cases are going to reach a wider audience than others. For example, your front-and-center, homepage explainer is going to be more important for your bottom line than your provider-side app onboarding video. You'll need to balance the cost of the video against its potential for helping your business.

But we're not done yet! Once you decide *how much* you want to pay, you'll need to decide to whom you want to pay it. There will be several competitors at every price point. How can you be sure you're picking the right one?

CHAPTER FIVE
TWENTY QUESTIONS
(PLUS FIVE MORE)

It's important to take the time to research several companies before jumping in, but what questions should you ask during this exploratory phase? Here's a list. Rip out this chapter and tack it to your wall. Unless you have the ebook version. Then just print it out. Screen repairs are expensive.

Let's focus on four aspects of a good explainer experience.

Logistics

How much does it cost? Beyond the sticker price, make sure to ask about their payment plans, revision charges, and any other hidden fees. Different companies have different methods of collecting payment, so make sure you have a solid understanding of the true cost.

Do you have alternative payment options? A 50% down payment is typical. Some companies will offer installment plans or paid-in-full upfront discounts.

How long does it take? Most companies will require at least three weeks to make a custom video from scratch. Some will require eight. Some will offer a rush service that can prioritize your project.

Are all your styles the same price? Be careful with companies that have too many criteria for their quotes. Additional charges for extra characters or backgrounds may be warning signs for hidden fees coming in the future.

Do you have overage charges? You'll typically be paying for a specific video length. Watch out for hidden clauses that will cost you if your video goes into overtime.

Are there any extra fees? Don't get tricked into paying more than you intended.

Creativity

What animation styles do you do? Don't get pigeonholed into doing just one style because the company doesn't offer others.

Will you be providing creative input? Or is it up to you to be the idea person? Find out the level of creative input you'll receive.

What's your production process? Do they include script writing? Storyboarding? Voiceover recording?

Who writes the script? What is their experience level and education? Do they have experience writing for all types of industries? Are they able to understand, or willing to do research on, complex processes that might be necessary for your video? Do they write comedy? Ask to see examples of their work, and see if they're fun and engaging, or dry and boring.

What are my voice actor options? Do they offer translation and voices in other languages or accents?

Credibility

How many videos have you made? Be wary of companies that cite a high number but only have a few in their portfolio.

How long have you been in business? New companies pop up all the time. They'll often pretend to be experienced. You don't really want to be client number one.

Where are you located? Google their address, go to street view. If it's somebody's house or a mailbox service, you might be dealing with an offshore freelancer in disguise.

Have you made videos for clients in my industry? Ask to see examples. If they've made videos for your industry, they're more likely to understand your needs, and that reduces your risk.

Have you made crowdfunding videos for successful campaigns? Even if you're not running a Kickstarter or Indiegogo campaign, this is a great way to quantify the success of their videos.

Service

Do you have any testimonials? See what other clients have said about them.

Can I call a past client for reference? If they can't dredge up at least three phone numbers for you, that's not a good sign.

How responsive are you? Are they available to be reached by phone? During what hours? Do they work every day of the week? How long does it take for them to get back to their clients? And don't just take their word for it. Before you sign up, take a few days corresponding with their team. Send them emails and see how long it takes for them to respond. Call in and see if someone picks up.

Who will be my contact during the process? Will you have a dedicated project manager? Are there others you can contact if you're not happy with their work or service?

Do you have written guarantees? Do they have a satisfaction guarantee that will allow you to cancel and protect your investment? What happens if the video you get isn't what you expected?

How many revisions can I make? Some companies will limit this to one or two rounds of changes, and will charge you a fee every time you make a revision request, even if it's due to poor work on their end. No company is going to get your video perfect the first time, so this never works out in your favor.

Do you help with video marketing? Do their responsibilities stop at production? There's a lot more to video marketing than just making the video. Will they help you get it out into the world, and help you get people to watch it and take action?

Can I make changes to the video after it's complete? Some companies will let you come back to them and make minor changes. Some won't allow it at all. Find out if they do, and how much it would generally cost. In my experience, it's almost inevitable that a video will need to be updated at some point, so plan for it as a certainty.

Will I own the completed video? Some companies will try to license your video to you, or host it on their own servers. Make sure you're receiving a download that is 100% yours, with no copyright limitations.

After you've found a production company at the right price point, with honest business practices, good reviews, and a portfolio you can get behind. It's time to bring your video to life. Soon, we'll peek behind the curtain and get a behind-the-scenes look at what it takes to create a great explainer video.

But first...can you sit down for a second? I need to talk to you.

CHAPTER SIX
THE TALK

Choosing your production company is a lot like dating, but with fewer disputes over who should pay the bill and uncomfortable half-hug-half-handshakes. So what a relief, you've finally exited the courtship phase, chosen a partner, and are ready to go steady. Now, as with any relationship, success relies on managing your expectations.

Finding balance. The production of explainer videos falls into a tricky gray area between art and business. Like a portrait painter or a studio movie director, explainer producers are constantly balancing the expectations of their clients with the limitations and ambitions of their artistry.

As you embark on the production process, you'll need to consider this balance as well. Explainer videos are art, and no good art ever came from artists being rushed, doted on, or put under undue pressure. However, this video is for your business, which makes every creative decision a business decision, and they should be treated as such.

Don't expect your production team to create a perfect video for you without your input—but also don't expect your input to be the only thing that matters. In my experience, the best videos are created when

> Don't expect your production team to create a perfect video for you without your input—but also don't expect your input to be the only thing that matters.

the production team and client develop a solid working relationship. The worst videos are created when the client can't be bothered to provide feedback, or when they never allow themselves to waiver from the exact vision they had starting out.

It's not all roses. In most cases, producing an explainer video will be a collaborative experience, and you'll quickly hit a stride with your project manager or point of contact. If all goes well, you'll be on the same page creatively, and the process will go smoothly. If it hits a snag, however, don't get discouraged. Hopefully you've chosen a company that allows you to revise the work, and you'll be there to guide your team back on track.

It's important to reconcile your expectations with the reality of the project. Your video is not going to look exactly like it looks in your head right now, but you should be able to get pretty close. Most of the time you'll be able to communicate to your team why something didn't meet your expectations and bring them closer to your vision.

Only fools rush in. Creating a custom video from scratch is a time-intensive process. Depending on the complexity of the project, It can take anywhere from two weeks to three months. The "I need it yesterday" mentality might lead to success in other parts of your business, but if you come into the video creation process with a tight deadline, you're going to have a bad time and might end up with a low-quality production.

Because video production is a collaborative and creative process, I never guarantee deadlines for our clients, and I'd be wary of any company that does. You just need time for the project to grow and adjust. But even if we could read a client's mind and somehow get everything right on the first attempt, video production still requires an incredible amount of time and labor. Remember, animation requires creating every frame of the video, then meticulously rigging, keyframing, and animating the different assets. Even highly-skilled animators will need a fair amount of time to complete this process.

So you want to write a viral video? Here's my advice. Don't. For every Dollar Shave Club, Dos Equis, and Squatty Potty, there are a million ads that attempted to make something ridiculous and over the top and fell flat on their face in the process. There's nothing worse than seeing a video that was clearly attempting to be a worldwide phenomenon hovering around 300 views.

A viral video is like a #1 song or box office smash hit. You can't control what's going to be popular; all you can do is guess. And if you don't already have an audience, the chances that you're going to make it to the top of the charts are slim.

> A viral video is like a #1 song or box office smash hit. You can't control what's going to be popular; all you can do is guess.

Focus on creating the best video you can. Use humor if you want, but don't throw everything at it in the hope that you'll break the Internet. The odds are you won't, and you'll still want your explainer to be valuable to the people who actually do watch it.

Okay. Wipe the sweat off your brow and take a deep breath, the tough love section of the book is over. We've successfully managed our expectations. Now we can start the project, right?

Not quite. In order for your production company to understand you, you will first have to understand yourself.

CHAPTER SEVEN
WHO
ARE YOU?

O ne of the most delightful side effects of the video production process, especially for new businesses, is that it encourages clients to examine their brand, products, and values. I've had more than one client express how helpful it was for them to sit down and really decide what they were all about.

Before your script can be written, you need to be able to answer some basic questions about who you are and what you do. To borrow a bit of wisdom from proto-how-to author Lao Tzu. "He who knows others is wise. He who knows himself is enlightened."

What is your product or service? It's important to be as specific as possible when answering this question. Do you want a video that promotes your entire business, or just one aspect of it? What will the consumer actually get if they choose you? Your product or service should have a specific name that's easy to remember. If you're promoting more than one product, what differentiates them?

What problems does it solve? Why does your product or service exist? What's its origin story? Why does a consumer need your product? What pain can it help alleviate? How are they worse off when they don't have you in their lives? How are they better off when they do have you in their lives?

What are the key features of your product or service? What are two or three unique advantages of using your product or service? If your company was a novel, what would be on the back of the book?

Who are your competitors? Think about direct and indirect competitors. Are you competing with other businesses? Other products? Are you competing with the idea of not using your product or service at all? How are you different from your competitors? How are you better? What can you offer the customer that they can't?

What is your brand? How do you want to be perceived? Is your company an austere protector? An authority figure? A friendly face?

What symbols and colors represent you? It's very important to create a video that aligns with this perception.

What is your message? If you could distill your brand down to one sentence, what would that be? How about one word? If someone only watched your video once, what one thing would you want them to understand about you?

Who is your target audience? How old are they? What gender? How much money do they have? How much do they already know about your business? What is their mindset when they are viewing your video? Are you targeting businesses or consumers? If you're targeting businesses, what level of seniority are you targeting? If you're targeting consumers, what other parts of your sales cycle will they already have been exposed to?

What action do you want the audience to take? Are you trying to close the sale? Or just trying to get the viewer more interested? Do you have other promotional materials you can direct them to? Is there a free service you can offer them right off the bat, like a quote, consultation, or brochure? How can you get them to reach out and give you their contact info?

What obstacles could keep them from taking that action? What concerns do your customers usually have? What might prevent them from choosing your company? How can you alleviate those concerns before they think of them?

How are you planning on using your video? How will it be distributed? Is it for your homepage, or are you planning on reaching out with it? Don't worry if you don't know all the answers—we'll get into this later in the book.

Feeling enlightened? Good! Let's get started.

CHAPTER EIGHT
EQUIPPED TO SCRIPT

The script is absolutely the most important element of the production process. How important? More important than breakfast is to your day. Everything starts here. Bad videos have been made from good scripts, but good videos have never been made from bad scripts. So, if you don't have any experience with script writing, how can you tell if you're working with gold or cow dung?

> Bad videos have been made from good scripts, but good videos have never been made from bad scripts.

An explainer video needs to do three things:

○ Explain a complex idea concisely

○ Tell a good story

○ Make the audience do something

Whether you're writing your script yourself or revising the work of your production company, this **comprehensive guide to writing an explainer video script** will help you get through the process.

How long is too long? In this field, a lot of fuss has been made about the science of attention spans. How long will the typical person watch a video before they check out? Some might tell you it's a "rule" not to make a video longer than sixty seconds, or ninety seconds, or two minutes. Here's the truth—the more interesting your video is, the longer people will watch it. Case in point: remember Kony 2012? That thing was like half an hour. The only real rule for deciding on length is this: take as long as you need to, don't take longer than you have to.

> The only real rule for deciding on length is this: *take as long as you need to, don't take longer than you have to.*

> **Pro Tip:** How can you tell how long your video will be based on your script? We use a simple measure of 150 words of voiceover per minute.

Succinct. Concise. Economical. The first goal of your explainer is to take a complex idea and explain it in an easy-to-understand way. This will be accomplished through a combination of voiceover and visuals.

We'll cover the visuals later, but as far as voiceover is concerned, the key to making your video more engaging is economy of language. Follow the advice of Thomas Jefferson, who said, "The most valuable of all talents is that of *never using two words when one will do.*" Don't use a big word where a short one will do. Use active verb tenses. Avoid excess repetition. The shorter you can get your script while still saying the same thing, the more value each word will have, and the more interesting your video will be.

Here's an example:

Original: "Bob is wondering what he can do to help his struggling business. Bob should consider getting an explainer video"

Better: "Bob's business needs help. He needs an explainer video"

And as an added bonus, trimming the lan
can be extraordinarily therapeutic. It feels ju
closet and donating old clothes. Trust me.

Choosing your words carefully can get yo
converting your pitch into a short video. The
be covered with storytelling and literary techn

> **Pro Tip:** The simplest way to effectively achieve an economy of words is to lose the adjectives and adverbs. "Bob walked briskly down the narrow street toward his client's unadorned office" may be fine for a novel, but for a script, "Bob went to see his client" works much better.

Story Time. It doesn't matter if you're selling a dental plan or a mobile game. A great video tells a story, even if you don't realize it.

In general, we employ a couple of standard formats for explainer scripts. The first uses a character or characters for the audience to relate to ("Meet Bob..."). The second uses the audience as a character ("Have *you* ever..."). No matter which you choose, it is important to carry the story through the rest of the video. Both formats go on to follow this simple formula.

Explainer Video Secret Formula

> Examples of problems → plea for a solution → presentation of solution → explanation of benefits / how it works → call to action.

Here's an example.

> "Bob's telescope company is struggling. He wants a great explainer video, but doesn't know anything about production. If only there were a great resource for Bob to use. Then, a neighbor lent him this book! It tells him everything he needs to know about explainer video production. Order yours today!"

But maybe not very interesting. So how do we spice it up?

...t like English class. The things that make an explainer script more interesting are the same things that make a novel interesting. So go find the analysis you did on literary devices in *Moby Dick*. Or, if you burnt that along with the rest of your memories from high school, refer to the following.

Simile and Metaphor. If you have a complex idea, sometimes the best way to explain it is to compare it, directly or indirectly, to a less complex idea. For example, if you're operating a financial exchange, you might compare it to a lemonade stand. One of our clients was having trouble explaining how his IT company could incrementally replace the components of an existing IT system to make it run smoother. We decided to compare it to an old car, replacing the parts bit by bit, until it became a slick racer.

Allusion. If your video seems boring, sometimes a great way to add some humor is to use cultural references. Call upon a famous fable, or book, or movie scene, to draw in your viewer. A great example of this is Goldilocks. You wouldn't believe how many different goals can be accomplished by replacing the components of this story. A recent client of ours had Goldilocks choosing between different styles of office furniture.

Anthropomorphism. Are you unsure if your audience will relate to your characters? Why not make your characters cute animals? Everybody loves cute animals. One client of ours, who was creating a video for restaurant software, made all of his characters pieces of toast. The result is a little funnier and a lot more engaging than the same video would have been with only people in it.

Suspense. If your video is meant to draw in potential clients to do more research about you, sometimes it's best to leave your video on a cliffhanger. How can we help you save a thousand dollars per year? You'll have to visit our website to find out.

Tone. Ask any English teacher and they'll probably tell you tone is the hardest literary device to master. It's the amorphous, ambiguous way in which language can evoke different emotions from the audience. It's important to make the tone of your video match your intentions. Will it be humorous? Dark? Emotional? Dry? You'll need to adjust the language accordingly.

Let's check in with Bob and see if we can make use of some of these tools.

"Bob knows his telescopes are out of this world! But sales have been less than astronomical, because Bob's website is like a black hole. Customers come in...and he never hears from them again. But then Bob saw a message in the stars. It said 'YOU NEED AN EXPLAINER VIDEO.' But while Bob can tell you Venus from Uranus on a cloudy day, he doesn't know anything about video production. If only there were a great resource for Bob to use. Well, Bob is in luck! This book tells him everything he needs to know about explainer video production. Order yours today!"

There. Isn't that better?

Tailor your script to fit. You're not going to successfully explain anything worthwhile from scratch in a short amount of time. You'll to need to draw upon the experiences of your target audience. And every audience is different and carries different experiences with them. Only in rare cases will writing for the most universal audience be the best strategy for your script.

For example, if your video is a pitch for investors, you're going to need to use the language of a business person. Don't waste time explaining what a return on investment is, just tell them how you're going to increase their ROI.

If you have a product or service that appeals to a few different groups of people, sometimes the best approach will be to create multiple videos that appeal to each audience separately, instead of lumping them all together. I might be mixing up my facts, but I'm pretty sure it was Confucius who said, "A video that tries to appeal to everyone, appeals to no one."

The call to action. Some might say this is the most important part of the script. This is where we'll see if all the effort pays off. Will your client click the link to learn more? Will they order your product today? Will they schedule a consultation? The suspense is killing me.

The three tools that you can use to convince someone to do something are called *modes of persuasion*. Aristotle invented them 2,300 years ago. In case you're like me, and missed the first day of public speaking class because of some bad dining hall chili, here's a quick rundown.

Ethos. This is when you appeal to the audience based on your credibility, or in this case, the credibility of your company. An example of an ethos-based call to action is: "So see why hundreds of customers have already chosen Cooler than Cucumbers Air Conditioning. Buy your unit today!"

Pathos. This is when you appeal to the emotions of the viewer. This can involve telling an emotionally compelling story to convince your audience to choose you. It can also involve telling them how good they might feel if they use your product or service, or how bad they might feel if they don't. An example of a pathos-based call to action is: "Now is the time to take control of your life. Sign up for the Melt-Away weight loss 90-day risk free trial."

Logos. This is when you use logic to make your point, and appeal to your viewer's sense of reason. An example of a logos-based call to action is: "Why not see how Sealed Shut Energy can cut your monthly bill by up to 25%? Schedule a free consultation."

Each mode of persuasion has value in certain situations. The trick is figuring out which will work best for your prospective customers.

> **Pro Tip:** If you're not sure which call to action is best, ask your production company to create multiple versions for some A/B testing.

I hope that I've provided you with the tools you need to write a decent script, or at least judge whether a script is good or bad. Time to do some art!

CHAPTER NINE
A THOUSAND WORDS
ABOUT PICTURES

You've got a script that communicates your idea, tells a good story, avoids extraneous language, and has a compelling call to action. Now it's time to decide how it should look.

If your script is like breakfast, the most important meal of the day, then choosing a video style is like an excessive, all-you-can-eat weekend lunch. You're going to be overwhelmed by options, not all of them will be healthy, and you're going to need to avoid over-indulging.

Let's take a stroll down the buffet and have a look at the entrées.

Your guide to explainer video styles.

Standard 2D Animation. Also called "cartoons." This style is usually full color, usually involves characters, and resembles what you saw on Saturday mornings growing up. The characters can be very goofy-looking, or very realistic. Standard 2D animation is a great choice for character-centered videos with a focus on story.

3D Animation. This is a pricier service that won't be offered by every production company. It involves making 3D models of the components of your video, and using special software to put them in a built environment with lighting.

> **Pro Tip:** I generally only recommend 3D animation if you're trying to demonstrate a very technical process with a high level of accuracy, or show off a fancy new gadget. If you just want 3D because you love Pixar movies, it's rarely worth the added cost.

Text-Based Animation. These are videos that have the entire script written out on screen in dynamically moving words. Many times, these videos won't have a voiceover to accompany them. They can be very powerful, and great for marketing on Facebook, where videos autoplay without sound.

Motion Graphics. This is similar to text based animation, but uses images, symbols, charts and graphs, as well as text, to get the point across. This style is perceived as being more "professional" than standard 2D animation and, if done right, can be very attractive. This is a great option for videos with a more serious tone, and for videos that are meant to appeal to a business or investor audience.

Hand Sketch. Also called "whiteboard videos," this style burst onto the scene sometime around 2009, and they are still very popular, leading some people to assert that they are overused. Many production companies only do videos in this style. They involve a hand drawing images on a whiteboard. The images themselves aren't generally animated, and the visual interest comes from watching the hand sketch them out.

There are two major types of whiteboard video. Real whiteboard videos are sped-up live shots of actual hands drawing on actual whiteboards, and are usually more expensive than computer generated whiteboard videos, which accomplish the same effect using software.

This can be a great style for videos with an educational tone. That being said, many view it as a trend, and unlike standard 2D animation or motion graphics, it has the potential to go out of style.

Live Action. Video of real people on real sets doing real things. As I wrote in chapter three, live action is a whole different animal, involving high costs and a very complex and involved production process. If you can afford it, however, a high-quality live action video can do wonders for your business.

Live Action/Animation Mix. Another option is to combine live action and animated elements. The most common variation of this style is to film an actor in front of a green screen, and insert animation over the background to create a more interesting or exciting presentation. This kind of style is great for Kickstarter videos, where the inventor/founder of the project is expected to have a presence.

Stock Footage. If you're really interested in doing a live action video, but can't afford the hefty price, you might want to look into using stock footage. Combining pre-made imagery of people doing activities related to your product or service with clever text or motion graphics can create a pretty convincing effect.

Animating Over Real Photos. Similar to the stock footage option, computer animation is extremely versatile, and can easily be combined with real photographs from other sources. For example, if you're a realtor trying to sell a property, you could take photographs of the property and have animated characters walking through it. This style is a great best-of-both-worlds solution for people who want a professional vibe but also cartoon characters.

Screencast/Screenshots. Another tool at your disposal is the screencast. This is a recording of a computer or phone screen that can be incorporated into a video, and is very useful for promoting software and apps.

How do you choose which of these styles to use? Do some of them perform better than others?

It comes down to the content of your script and your target audience. Take the time to put yourself in their shoes and imagine what they'd like to see. More professional audiences, or companies promoting more serious products or services, will tend to benefit from a motion graphics video. Videos targeting children or families, or that are working with a more humorous or light-hearted script, will benefit from 2D "cartoon" animation.

> **If you still aren't sure what style your video should be, here are some things you can do:**
>
> O Ask people whose opinions you trust
>
> O Watch a lot of sample videos
>
> O Ask your production company for recommendations based on your brand

Once you've chosen a video style, your production company will create a storyboard for you, with your script broken down into scenes and accompanied by initial sketches of your animation. This is followed by illustrations, where you'll finally get to see what your video will look like! It's important to review the illustrations and make sure that they're the building blocks of a great video.

How to make your illustrations really pop

Play off of your voiceover. During this phase of production, you should constantly refer to your voiceover script to make sure that the illustrations are complementing it nicely. In general, you'll want your visuals to be conveying separate information from your voiceover in order to double down on the amount of information in your video. Using visual metaphors or charts and graphs are great ways to accomplish this. However, for some important moments of your script, it's okay to just write out your voiceover text in big bold letters for emphasis.

Incorporate your branding. Aligning your video style with the overall branding of your company is a great way to expand on your brand and protect your video from theft. If you have company colors, use them as motifs throughout the video. Make sure your logo is present. You might consider using it as a watermark that appears throughout the video as well. If you've had any other graphic design work done, be sure to share it with your production team, so they can use it as a reference.

Character design is key. If you have characters in your video, you should have a handle on how you'd like them to be drawn. Stick figures and similar amorphous or ambiguous characters can communicate an "everyman" quality, and are potentially more relatable. Cartoon styles resembling those of beloved animation studios, like Disney or Looney Tunes, can recall pleasant memories in the minds of your audience and imbue your video with a happier tone. Very realistic characters, on the other hand, can add an air of sophistication to your video.

Remember your Mise-en-scène. This is a hoity-toity film school phrase that basically refers to all the information within a frame. In your video, everything from the setting to the colors to the lighting will communicate something to your audience. Don't waste an opportunity to pack more information in.

For example, if you're marketing a sleep aid and you're showing a character who can't sleep in their bedroom, you might want to make their bed all messy, clothes all over the floor, etc. to demonstrate their anguished mental state. That's mise-en-scène.

In addition, don't forget about your characters' hair, makeup, and costumes, and use the overall video setting, including time of day and weather, to your advantage.

Add a couple of sight gags. Your illustrations can add humor to your video, even when viewed independently from your voiceover script. In Hollywood, purely visual jokes are called "sight gags." These can be anything from a sign or bumper sticker with a funny phrase on it, to a little bit of slapstick action between your characters. One of my favorite kinds of sight gag is when a character interacts with an on-screen element that the audience doesn't expect them to see, for example, jumping out of the way of a rapidly incoming logo and phone number.

Once your illustrations are complete, it's time to compile your final video. It will seem like just yesterday that this project was just a spark of an idea in your head. Over the past few weeks, you've watched it blossom into a full grown production. Now, you're about to send it off to face this big, bad world...

Stop. There's no time to be sentimental. We've got a ways to go yet.

CHAPTER TEN
SOUND JUDGMENT

I t's tantalizingly close now. So close you can taste it. The script is perfect. Every frame has been illustrated. Any minute now that video is going to come through the pipes and you'll finally get to see the product of all this hard work.

Your animation team will be painstakingly rigging each component of your video and adding motion and effects. This is a meticulous process that will take some time.

While they're working, there's just a few things left for you, the client, to consider, and each deserves just as much care and thought as you've given to the rest of the process. These final tasks have to do with those big funny-looking things on the sides of your face.

Sound is almost as important to your video as imagery. Great sound can make your video come alive in the minds of the viewer. Not-so-great sound can make your video feel extremely unprofessional.

There are three major components for you to worry about: Voiceover, Music, and Sound Effects.

Voiceover-Easy. This is the narration of your video. A typical explainer video will have one voiceover actor reading your script, but you might also be including dialogue, with multiple actors. In either case, choosing the right actor, or actors, is imperative.

Always use a professional voice actor, or at least professional equipment. Unless you have access to a recording studio, or a studio-quality microphone and software, recording the voiceover yourself is a bad idea. Poor audio quality is obvious, and will undo all the hard work put into making your video seem well put-together. Plus, it's not as easy as it sounds to imbue every line of your script with drama and energy, and professional voice actors are experienced at doing just that.

> Unless you have access to a recording studio, or a studio-quality microphone and software, recording the voiceover yourself is a bad idea.

Many production companies will have voice actors on staff, or existing relationships with voice actors, and they'll show you their samples so you can make a choice of what sound works best for you. If you're responsible for finding your own voice actor, there are many marketplaces online where you can hire professionals to read your script.

But which actor should you choose? You'll be choosing based on three criteria: gender, age, and accent. Obviously, an old British man's voice is going to have a different effect on your video than a young American woman's.

Gender. People say that male voices are perceived as more forceful and convincing, while female voices are perceived as nurturing and trustworthy. I have absolutely no idea if this is true.

A 2010 Adweek/Harris Poll survey[1] found that 18% of respondents found a male voice more persuasive, while 19% of respondents

---

[1] *Are Consumers More Responsive to Male or Female Voices in Advertisements?* Harris Poll, 2010

said a female voice was. The rest said it made no difference. These results are, of course, inconclusive, and prove the point that the voice of one gender is not necessarily better for your video than the other.

You'll need to consider what you're selling, and to whom you are selling it, and use your best judgment. For example, it would be kind of strange to have a man's voice in a video for your better brassiere invention. It would be equally strange to have a woman's voice advertising a 5-blade men's razor. For every scenario in between, just go with your gut.

Age. There are no data on the subject that I can find, but I am inclined to believe that an older-sounding voice is more likely to be described as wiser and more authoritative than a younger sounding voice. On the other hand, youthfulness and energy are great tools for selling a product or service. So we come to another crossroads. I'm afraid the answer is, again, to use your best judgment. If you have a product targeting older people, it makes sense to use an older voice. If you want to be perceived as cool and edgy, then a young person's voice will suit you better.

Accent. This problem is easier to tackle. In almost every case, it's wise to use the same accent as the region you're targeting, because if someone hears an accent other than their own, they might have a feeling that the video isn't for them. For example, I would be rightly confused if a Cockney British voice was telling me about a lawn care company in Idaho.

> **Pro Tip:** Consider using a foreign accent if you're going for some kind of special effect. For example, I had a client who played on the tropes of a nature documentary in their video, so even though they were an American company, they decided to go with a rugged Australian voice.

If you have a product or service that you're selling all over the English-speaking world, then the situation gets trickier. Once again, the data set is thin. A study published in the Journal of Global Marketing[2] found that when tested against a local accent (Singaporean, in this case), British accents were perceived as more credible. I'm inclined to believe this might be true when tested against other accents as well, but we can't be certain.

A less formal survey published by Time Out showed that British accents were listed as "sexiest," with three times as many votes as the second place finisher[3]. Unless you're selling lingerie, this result won't be very helpful. I recommend sticking with the three major English-speaking accents (British, American, Australian), and from there, using your best judgment.

---

[2] *Consumer Responses to English Accent Variations in Advertising*, Journal of Global Marketing, 2003

[3] *Time Out's Global Dating Survey results are revealed!*, Time Out, 2015

Elevated Music. Get ready for some heartbreak. You're not allowed to use "Stairway to Heaven," "Total Eclipse of the Heart," *or* the "Imperial March" from *Star Wars* to soundtrack your explainer video. In fact, you're not allowed to use any unlicensed copyrighted material.

At least in the USA, explainer videos promoting products or services are not protected by fair use. Even if they were, all the major hosting sites, like YouTube, have algorithms that automatically detect copyrighted music and will remove your video from the site if it's in violation of the law.

So unless you have the capital to buy the rights to your favorite song, or have a musician friend that will lend you their talents, you're going to need to use royalty-free or "stock" music. There are a few websites that have royalty-free music libraries where everything is simply free. Others will require you to give them credit, or attribution. Some will have larger libraries, and allow you to license their music for a small fee.

Music sets the mood in a video. In fact, those libraries I mentioned will often be organized by mood. "Uplifting," "dramatic," "upbeat," and "fun" are words you'll be seeing over and over. Try to choose something that isn't distracting, and matches the tone of your video. If you can watch your video without really noticing the music, then you're probably on the right track.

The Sound Effect Effect. Check in with your production company to see if they offer sound effects as part of their service. If they do, make sure to request them. If they don't, hire a sound designer to do them after the fact. If they are at an extra cost, pay it.

The effect that sound design will have on your video is immense. It's the most important thing you don't know you're missing. Every *plunk*, *bloop*, and *ka-ching* will add a layer of depth and dimension to your video.

Be careful, it's possible to go overboard. Poorly mixed or excessive sound effects will have the opposite effect on your video. But when they're done right, they work wonders.

～

And just like that, your video is done! What a journey it's been. From script to illustrations to animation to sound, you've gone from the seed of an idea to a real, finished thing that actually exists! Take a moment and revel in the feeling of success. Send a gift basket to your production company (I really like gourmet chocolate with hazelnuts and whiskey).

So now that your video's done...

CHAPTER ELEVEN
WHAT THE HECK DO
I DO WITH IT?

Your video has the potential to help grow your business, increase your conversions, increase your visibility, and expand your reach. But it's not going to do any of this on its own. You're going to need to do some heavy lifting in hosting it, implementing it, and putting your video in all the best places to maximize your return on investment.

Think of your video like King Kong. Right now, he's on Skull Island, fighting dinosaurs, doing his thing, but there's no inherent value in a 60-foot gorilla. It's your job to bring him to New York, promote the act, and charge tickets to see him. Except that your video isn't going to escape, kill a bunch of people, and climb the Empire State Building. Okay, maybe this was a bad example.

There are tons of ways to make use of your new video! Let's go over a few of them.

Marketing Star! Move over, Paula from IT, your video will be your new employee of the month. It works 24/7, doesn't require coffee, and can talk to a million clients at once. How can you beat that? Here are a few great avenues for using your video to reach out to prospective clients.

Put it on your homepage. This is the most obvious route. Slap that baby front and center on your website, so that your visitors can get your message right away, instead of having to sift through boring text. These days, it is pretty much expected that any business worth its salt is going to have a video somewhere on its homepage.

Attract visitors the way you always have, with ads or other outreach campaigns, and if they show interest, the first action they'll take on your site is watching your video, providing them with the incentive to take action.

Another great web tool is a landing page. This is a focused web page which contains just your video, some basic information, and a highly desirable offer or lead magnet. If you're launching a new product and your video doesn't belong on your homepage, setting up a landing page for it is easy, and might be just what you need.

> **Pro Tip:** Use unique landing pages for your different audiences or customer segments to maximize conversions. And for even better performance over time, use Optimizely or Visual Website Optimizer to run A/B split tests.

Advertise on YouTube, Facebook, and Instagram. All three of these services allow you to advertise your video to your exact audience, so they are great places to reach new customers. You probably won't be able to use your homepage explainer on these because of its length. An ideal video ad is just 15-40 seconds long. However, your production company might be able to re-cut a shorter version of your video for an additional fee. Many of my clients will order a 15-second commercial to accompany their main explainer for exactly this reason, so we offer this service at just a small extra cost.

Advertising on these services is sort of like advertising on TV, just a gazillion times better. You can target your ad to only reach users searching keywords relevant to your audience. For example, if you've developed a car cleaning product, you can choose to only target users searching automotive related keywords. You can also target users based on their personal information (occupation, age, gender, etc.).

The reach is practically limitless. YouTube is the largest video site in the world, and the second most used search engine after Google. Facebook and Instagram are the largest social media sites. You have the potential to find clients who would never have found you otherwise.

Plus, with these ad services, you only pay for ads if clients watch all the way through, and don't pay anything if they skip. How cool is that?

Perhaps best of all, you can use video advertisements to "retarget" people who have already visited your site, leading to fewer missed opportunities and increasing conversions. The fact is that most visitors to your website will leave without taking action, but that doesn't mean they aren't interested. Retargeting lets you follow up with these missed connections. You'll also be building your brand and credibility in the process, as potential customers will think you're a big player when they see your advertisement on all the most popular websites.

> The fact is that most visitors to your website will leave without taking action, but that doesn't mean they aren't interested.

Enhance your social media presence. There's a good chance that, on the advice of a marketing consultant, friend, or nagging business partner, you've gone ahead and set up Facebook, Instagram, Twitter, YouTube, and maybe even a Pinterest account for your business. There's an equally good chance that you have absolutely no idea what to post on those accounts, and that a few of them have been dormant since a week after activation. Well, here's a golden opportunity to wake them back up again!

Video is built for social media. Post your explainer on all your social pages, and encourage your followers to share it. If it's an interesting enough video, people will share it just because they think it's interesting, providing you with free advertising and the ability to go viral. On Facebook and Twitter, you have the choice to pin posts to keep them at the top of your page and increase visibility. Your video is a great post to pin.

Send it in an email campaign. Unlike most of the relics of the early Internet, email is still thriving as a mode of communication and advertising. If you already use an email marketing service, it's a great idea to create a new campaign with your video as the star. If you don't already use an email marketing service, now's a great time to start! While email integration with video isn't superb, there are a few methods for connecting them. One of the best is putting a mock play button or thumbnail in the body of the email and linking it to your video's hosting site.

Putting the Fun in Fundraising. Explainer videos aren't just great for selling products and services that already exist. They're also great for promoting the ideas that you still need funding to create! Whether it's through the power of the crowd, or more traditional methods of raising capital, video can help turn your dreams into reality.

Crowdfunding ain't easy. And without a video, it's damn near impossible. Go ahead and find me one successful Kickstarter or Indiegogo campaign that didn't have a video on their page. Kickstarter and its contemporaries have broken down the barriers between a great idea and the marketplace, but even the best ideas still need good pitches to sell 'em. Let your explainer video be that pitch.

People don't just throw their hard-earned money at ideas without some convincing, and we've already discussed the persuasive power of video and the credibility it adds for your business. Plus, a really good explainer is more likely to be shared on social media, which is the key to gaining traction for your campaign and meeting or surpassing your goals.

Investors are people too. Which means, just like the rest of us, they probably don't like sitting in a room being talked at for hours on end. You already know, that to raise money from venture capitalists and their kin, you're going to need to spice up your sales pitch.

When you worked on your video script, you took all the best things about your idea and boiled them down into the most effective, succinct, condensed version of themselves. Why would you revert back to plain old talking aloud when you've got such a valuable asset in your back pocket? Leading your sales pitch off with a video will increase your chances of attracting interest.

Video isn't just for the Internet. Your business exists in the
physical world as well as the digital one, so why not take your video with you to the places you do business?

If you have a brick and mortar store, you can set up a monitor and put your video on loop. I had a customer who used this strategy to promote his flooring product on the sales floor. He set up a little kiosk next to the inventory where people could watch the video and learn a little bit about it.

If you do trade shows, video can be a great tool to make your booth stand out from the others. It catches people's eye and will make them stand in front of you long enough to start a conversation.

> **Pro Tip:** If you travel to other offices for sales meetings, keep your video on a flash drive and always keep it with you. It can be like your personal sales assistant!

Explainer videos are also great for delivering any kind of briefing that you would generally train an employee to give. We've had clients use our service to create safety spiels for everything from factory tours to trampoline parks.

Internal Affairs. Video doesn't have to be just outward-facing, either. It can help your business anywhere you could use a little more engagement. For example, training new hires, or informing your existing employees about new strategies or policy changes. Explainer videos can also be great tutorials for software, hardware, or any other kind of ware.

In the long run, your explainer video can actually *lower* your costs, by eliminating the need for employees to do repetitive tasks such as training personnel.

Test the Waters. Video can also be a great tool for selling something that doesn't exist. Not in a scammy kind of way, but in a market research kind of way.

Remember how video makes you seem serious about a product or service? If you have an idea, but aren't sure how people will react, a great strategy is to create a video and a landing page, then analyze how many conversions you get on an action like signing up for a waiting list. Even though video requires an investment to create, it can actually save you money in the long run, by letting you test whether an idea is viable before you take any steps toward bringing it to market.

When used properly, video can be the best employee you ever hired. And with so many uses for it, you might consider doing more than one.

CHAPTER TWELVE
THE HOST WITH THE MOST

Time to stop the tour for a second for a technical digression. Before you can put your video out in the world, you'll need to host the video somewhere. Your hosting service is where your video file will actually live, and how viewers will access it. It's important to understand that just because a video appears somewhere, that doesn't necessarily mean it's hosted there.

Most of the time, videos are hosted in servers of hosting companies, and then embedded in other places. There are several options for hosting, some of which will be familiar to you, and some that are more specialized. We're going to break down the big four.

Self-Hosting. The most obvious place to host your video is on your own website. You host the rest of your content here, so why not your video? There are a few reasons why this can be a bad move.

First, you're paying for real estate on your website's servers. Whether you use Amazon Web Services or a different web host, you're being charged for the amount of storage and connectivity you need, and videos are generally BIG files. This spells bad news for your monthly rates. Large videos without proper bandwidth and storage considerations can cause your site to load slowly, and even crash if too many users try to access it at once.

Second, there are other technical considerations which your self-hosting plugin might not be able to handle, like converting video for viewing in different web browsers, or on mobile. If you're not careful, this could lead to some potential customers getting an error message in place of your awesome new explainer.

Finally, if you self-host, you're missing out on some of the major benefits of external hosting, like the ability to learn valuable information about your viewers.

Best For: No one. With so many free hosting options, self-hosting is not a good idea in any scenario.

YouTube. YouTube is the largest hosting service in the world, and the second most visited website overall. This is many people's first thought for video hosting, as it's already a familiar part of our Internet routine. You'll definitely want to put your video on YouTube, but not only on YouTube.

The first reason to use YouTube is advertising. As we discussed in the previous chapter, YouTube is a great place to reach new audiences. YouTube advertisements take the form of videos that play automatically before other videos - so in order to use this service, you'll need to host the video on YouTube.

YouTube is a video network, which means people browse the site and use it as a search engine, increasing the chances that potential customers will stumble upon your company's video on their own, without having been directed there by an advertisement. YouTube is also owned by Google, which means it gains preferential treatment in search listings. Putting your video up on YouTube allows you to capitalize on these advantages, and it's free, so you've got nothing to lose.

However, for embedding the video *on your website*, you're going to want a different host. YouTube is supported by ad revenue, and therefore has one goal—to direct visitors back to YouTube. They accomplish this through several means, including autoplay and recommended videos. So right after your video finishes playing, when you need your potential customers to be considering your call to action, they'll instead be greeted with nine similar videos to watch next, some of which may just be from your competitors.

> **Best For:** Google and YouTube search rankings and YouTube advertising. Not ideal for embedding videos on your website.

Vimeo and Wistia. For hosting videos on your website, you'll want to use a service like Vimeo or Wistia. These companies offer free plans that limit number of videos and bandwidth, and affordable paid plans that allow you to upload more videos and unlock extra features.

Because these services are not ad-supported, they do not try to lead people back to their own platforms. This makes them ideal for embedded hosting, as you know people won't be stolen away after finishing your video. In fact, both services actually offer lead generation features that allow you to collect email addresses and contact info directly in the video frame.

These services also offer analytics and customization. Analytics will allow you to gain insight into how people are reacting to your video, how long they watch, and when they decide to click away. Wistia also allows you to change the color of your video player, and even upload versions of your video with different beginnings and endings to allow for A/B testing.

Best For: Embedding on your website, Analytics, Customization.

Picking the right hosting service will help everyone see your video, but won't necessarily play the same to every audience. If you're considering expanding your business to other parts of the world, you're going to need to adapt your video accordingly.

CHAPTER THIRTEEN
LOCALIZATION
COMPLICATIONS

The Internet is a miracle. At no other time in history could a small business expand into global markets so easily. And sometimes, in the current economic climate, becoming a global business is not just a possibility—it's a necessity. "We live in a global economy." How many times have you heard politicians say that? And they have a point. It is a global economy, so in order to compete, you're going to need a *global* market share.

There are all sorts of reasons to expand into foreign markets. There might be less competition, or greater revenue streams. But how do you go about transitioning your web presence to suit other countries? All you need are a few translations, and *bing bang boom*, you're selling in China. Or Brazil. Or Timbuktu. Right?

Unfortunately, it's not so easy. Some components of your business strategy won't translate so well into other markets without additional effort. Video is one of these components.

Let's find out **how to adapt your explainer video for foreign markets.**

In some cases, *simply translating your video will be enough.* However, translating a video is not so simple.

Your production company might offer translation and foreign language voiceover services. If they don't, they may be able to take a foreign voiceover you provide and edit your video accordingly. Part of the issue of translating video is that the animation will usually need to be re-cut to match the pacing of the foreign language narration. Swift, punchy moments where words and their corresponding images lined up exactly in the English language version won't make sense any more, and will need re-working. Any text within the graphics of your video will need to be translated also. All this work can increase the costs for each translation.

> **Pro Tip:** A much cheaper option for translating is subtitling your video in different languages. However, if you do this, you risk being perceived as not serious about gaining business in foreign markets. How would you feel, for example, if a Chinese company expected you to watch their videos in Mandarin with English subtitles?

Sometimes, *adapting video for foreign markets requires more than just translation.* The imagery, concepts, and execution will all need to be changed as well.

It will be costly to create a unique version of your video for every market you enter. However, when compared against the potential gains, these costs might be worthwhile.

Video components that might need to be reworked include:

Cultural references. Do you remember in the script chapter when I told you about that client who made a video following the format of "Goldilocks and the Three Bears"? That's an example of a video that might not make any sense overseas. References to your country's myths, folklore, and pop culture are going to need to be edited for foreign use.

Sensitive material. Some cultures are more conservative than others. This can become problematic, because we offer up characters and situations and ask the viewer to imagine themselves as those characters in those situations. So if you're selling a financial service that promises a healthy retirement, and your image of a healthy retirement is a man driving a motorboat with his wife wearing a bikini, that might not play so well in a country like Saudi Arabia or the UAE.

Race. Because the characters in your videos are often meant to act as surrogates for your viewers, it is important to consider the skin color of your viewers. If you're trying to sell a product in Ghana, or India, or Japan, having a video with all white characters probably won't get you very far.

Geography. In a similar note as the above, tailor the situations in your video to match the geography of the target country. Don't have people on sunny beaches in a video for Scandinavia. Don't have people skiing in a video for South Africa.

As your business expands, it will be up to you to decide which markets you want to enter. Wherever they are, it's important to take these items into consideration.

CONCLUSION

I know it can really stink being confronted with new realities and constantly catching up to advancing technology in order to stay relevant. But the age of the explainer video is here, so why not view this as an opportunity? Who knows, you just might learn a thing or two about your business along the way.

The good news is, you're armed to the teeth with knowledge. Congratulations! You are now officially an expert on explainer video production. That is, of course, if you actually read the book. Which I hope you did. I worked really hard on it.

Now that you know why you need an explainer, how to choose a production company, how to ensure it's a high quality video, and how to put it in action, you're as ready as you'll ever be to take the leap.

Knowing as much as you do, any production company would be lucky to have you as a client. I encourage you to do your research and shop around.

But I want to ask one favor from you. Please put Promoshin.com on your list. Call in and test us out! I think we'll exceed your standards.

ABOUT THE AUTHOR

Ever since he was an 18-year-old entrepreneur, Ben Marvazi has understood the power of marketing and how it can make or break a business.

Not only have Ben's past businesses benefited from his expertise, he has also helped a diverse array of companies successfully acquire leads and new clients using direct response marketing strategies. As a Google AdWords Certified Partner, Ben has profitably managed tens of millions of dollars in paid ad campaigns.

Today, his company Promoshin.com helps businesses around the world effectively communicate their message with tailor-made explainer videos at the most affordable prices and highest level of customer service. No wonder Promoshin.com has become the highest-volume animation studio on the web.

Clients range from bootstrapped startups to major companies like the Better Business Bureau, QuickBooks, Genentech, and Cisco.

Ben lives in sunny Los Angeles, and is passionate about entrepreneurship, marketing, startups, and traveling the world. He's visited and lived in over 30 countries, and hopes to see many more.

Contact: ben@promoshin.com

Promoshin

animated explainer video production

www.promoshin.com

.

Made in the USA
San Bernardino, CA
05 May 2017